Original title:
I Thought I Saw a Snowman Move

Author: Lorenzo Barrett
ISBN HARDBACK: 978-9916-94-260-4
ISBN PAPERBACK: 978-9916-94-261-1

A Snowy Illusion Revealed

In the yard, a figure stands,
Dressed all in frosty brands.
Gazing wide with button eyes,
Is it magic? What a surprise!

Then it jiggles, gives a shimmy,
Could it be? Never so slimmy.
Laughter bubbles, snowflakes spin,
Was that a wave? Or just a grin?

Rumors in the Snowflakes

Whispers float on winter's breeze,
Tales of snowmen, if you please.
Some swear they saw one glide and sway,
Others giggle, 'Nah, no way!'

Footprints lead to snowy mounds,
This one's dancing, can you hear the sounds?
Sledders pause, then burst with cheer,
As the snowy jig draws near!

The Cold Embrace of Mystery

Midst the flakes, a shape does prance,
With all the kids, it starts to dance.
Gloves in the air, top hat askew,
Did that fellow just shout out 'Boo'?

Frosty curls and a carrot nose,
But wait, is that a gust of prose?
Chasing laughter, tumbling feet,
It's snowman fun down the snowy street!

Faceless Wanderer of the Snowdrifts

On drifts high, a shadow looms,
With frosty charm, it spins and zooms.
No face to see, just a silly stance,
Can a snowman really prance?

It hops around the snowy pile,
Causes giggles and big old smiles.
While snowflakes dance to quirky tunes,
Who knew winter could make us swoon?

A Maze of White Ghosts

In a field of frosty glow,
Where chilly whispers play,
A snowman with a cheeky grin,
Decided on a frosty day.

With a hat that danced so bright,
And buttons made of coal,
He twirled and spun in sheer delight,
A jolly, funny soul.

His carrot nose escaped the freeze,
And wiggled left and right,
As giggles echoed through the trees,
A snowy frolic's flight.

Chasing shadows all around,
That snowball with a glee,
Suddenly the laughter found,
A merry jubilee!

Silhouettes Beneath the Snowfall

Beneath the flakes of swirling dance,
A figure starts to sway,
With arms that wave like they're entranced,
In a fluffy, white ballet.

A top hat placed upon his head,
In mischief, there he beams,
Was he alive, or just a shred
Of children's snowy dreams?

With every gust, he seems to shift,
And chuckles float on air,
Is that a snowman, or a gift
From winter's playful fair?

As giggles ripple through the night,
Those frosty friends unite,
For every snowman feels so light,
In laughter's pure delight!

Chilled Secrets of the Flurries

In the white, a figure stands,
Nose of carrot, twiggy hands.
But wait, did that hat just sway?
Or am I just lost in play?

The scarf flutters in the breeze,
Whispers chill among the trees.
Giggles echo through the frost,
As we wander, not a cost.

A laugh escapes, a jolly snicker,
Was that a move or was it quicker?
The chill on cheeks meets joy in eyes,
As frosty friends share silly sighs.

Mysteries hid in snowy heaps,
Behind each mound, a secret peeks.
With every snowflake, tales unfold,
In laughter, winter's magic told.

Whirlwinds and Wonder

Spinning snowflakes dance and sway,
As if they’ve come out to play.
Round and round in chilly swirl,
Could it be? A frosty twirl?

Laughter tumbles through the air,
As snowballs fly without a care.
A hat on fire, a button's grin,
Maybe frosty friends join in?

A gust of wind, and oh! What luck,
A snowy friend gets quite unstuck.
With a wiggle and a shake,
Do we laugh for fun's own sake?

Curiosity wraps 'round tight,
What is that? A gleam, a fright?
In winter's joy, we find the cheer,
A wonderland drawing near.

The Frosty Watcher

Perched upon a mound so high,
With coal-black eyes that seem to spy.
A frosty grin, a chilly stare,
What secrets hide beneath that hair?

Shivers run when laughter's near,
As snowflakes twinkle, bright and clear.
Did that button wink with glee?
Or is it just your eyes, not me?

With a twist and a springy bounce,
The frosty figure starts to pounce.
Is it real or are we dreaming?
In winter's jest, we hear it scheming.

Oh, the joy that winter brings,
Wrapped in jokes and funny flings.
With a wave, the snowman seems to sway,
Inviting us to join the play.

A Winter's Tale Unraveled

Tales of winter flutter out,
From every snowflake, twist, and shout.
Here a grin, there a wave,
In frosty realms, we misbehave.

Underneath that snowy cap,
Lies the secret of the hap.
What’s that movement near the tree?
Just a laugh? Or a mystery?

Snowballs fly with joyous cheer,
As our snowy pal draws near.
With each twirl, more giggles spark,
In the warmth of winter’s dark.

With every twist, the stories grow,
A snowy dance, a winter show.
In laughter’s glow, the night ignites,
Winter’s charm warms chilly nights.

Serpentine Figures in the Snow

In the frosty field they wiggled,
A jolly dance with shovels jiggled.
With carrot noses all a-twitch,
They shimmied by, oh what a glitch!

The kids all gasped, their eyes went wide,
As snowmen swirled, they couldn't hide.
A top hat tipped, a scarf went flying,
In laughter sweet, the cold winds sighing.

With arms outstretched, they weaved and spun,
Creating fun 'til day was done.
As evening fell, the moonlight blinked,
These frosty folks, so mischievous, winked.

So next time snowflakes start to fall,
Watch closely, blink, and you might sprawl.
For in the chill, the magic brews,
Where snowmen dance and nothing snooze!

The Frozen Whisper of Existence

Amidst the white where shadows play,
The frosty forms begin their sway.
With silent giggles, crisp and clear,
They prance along, spreading cheer.

Lumps of snow with hats so round,
Move ever so slyly, without a sound.
A wink here, a jiggle there,
What’s this frolic? Are they aware?

In the glow of the twilight hue,
Snowmen gossip, sharing the view.
Each flake a secret, a well-kept tale,
As snowy figures begin to sail.

Peeking out from a snow-draped tree,
Join the fun, it’s wild and free.
Those frosty whispers in moonlit glow,
Ensure astoundment in the snow!

Ethereal Echoes in the Snowdrifts

In the hush of a winter night,
Snowmen giggle, what a sight!
With twinkling eyes and joyful cheer,
Who knows what’s lurking 'round here?

A corn-cob pipe stood tall and proud,
As snowflakes danced, forming a crowd.
They wobbled and jiggled, feeling spry,
Chasing each other as they fly.

Every tumble and every slip,
Turns into laughter, a merry trip.
With frozen glee, they caper about,
As children marvel and jump, shout!

Underneath the starlit sky,
Do they whisper secrets? Oh my!
These frosty friends in the moonlight play,
Reminding us to laugh and sway.

The Magical Stillness of the Night

In the silence where snowflakes fall,
Snowmen plot; oh, hear them call.
With gentle twirls and muffled cheer,
Their frosty forms are drawing near.

With snowy hats and buttons bright,
They conspire through the starry night.
A little jig and a playful shove,
These frosty fellows are full of love.

Giggling softly, they leap with glee,
As winter's chill wraps cheerily.
Their eyes aglow in moonlit sheen,
A magical sight, so serene.

So nestle close, make a wish or two,
For snowmen dreams come true, it’s true!
They’ll twirl and spin till morning light,
In the stillness of this frosty night!

Dance of the Snowy Apparition

In the moonlight, a figure swayed,
Snowflakes around it gently played.
A twirl, a swirl, a jolly jig,
Was it magic, or just a twig?

Laughter echoed in the chill,
As it danced on the frosty hill.
With carrot nose and button eyes,
A frosty friend, oh what a surprise!

The snow people joining in the fun,
Twisting, spinning, one by one.
A winter's eve of whimsy bright,
Raising spirits with delight!

So if you glimpse a frosty waltz,
Don't fret or think it’s someone’s faults.
Just join the dance, don’t be shy,
In the snowy world, we all can fly!

The Silent Guardian of the Bluffs

On the edge of the icy slope,
A statue stands, a winter hope.
It guards the hills with quiet grace,
Smiling wide, snow on its face.

Its arms are wide, a frozen hug,
Telling tales with a gentle shrug.
With every gust, it seems to grin,
As if waiting for fun to begin.

Children giggle as they parade,
Around their guardian, unafraid.
With snowballs ready and hearts so bold,
Every snowfall is pure gold!

Whispers float on the frosty air,
"Did it move? Maybe, beware!"
But in the laughter, we just see,
A friend who loves our company!

Phantoms in the Winter Landscape

Among the trees, shadows glide,
Whirling gracefully, side to side.
Could it be just a playful breeze,
Or snowmen dancing with such ease?

In winter's night, the giggles rise,
As frosty flurries fill the skies.
A snowball fight, a comical scene,
With snow spirits so light and keen.

A hat tipped low, a scarf that twirled,
Beneath the stars, they swayed and whirled.
Do we dare to join their song?
Tripping along, we all belong!

So join the fun on this chilly night,
Silly shadows in frosty light.
Embrace the wonder, take a chance,
In this snowy realm, let's dance!

Curiosity in the Cold

A soft crunch beneath our feet,
What's that? A whisper, a beat?
A snowman winks with cheeky glee,
"Come closer and play with me!"

Poking and prodding, what's the plan?
Is it just me or is it a man?
A jolly laugh from the frosty mound,
Makes us giggle at the sound.

With every step, we dance around,
Frozen friends on snowy ground.
Mysteries melt in frosty air,
Curiosity, beyond compare!

As the moon rises, stars appear,
We leave with memories, oh so dear.
In the night, we say goodbye,
To our snowy pal, who seemed to fly!

Murmurs Beneath the Powdered Surface

In the yard, a frosty mound,
With a carrot nose, without a sound.
What was that? A wink, a grin?
Surely fun is about to begin!

Snowflakes giggling, a chilly cheer,
Laughter echoing, winter's clear.
Did it just wiggle? Oh, what a sight!
Frozen mischief under the moonlight!

Sleds are zipping, laughter grows,
Whispers carried by the gentle blows.
Elves on skis, in the glow they weave,
Frosty jesters make you believe!

But at dawn, the magic's gone,
Was it all just a silly con?
Yet the laughter lingers, isn't it grand?
The snowman chuckles, not so bland!

Frosty Whispers in the Night

Beneath the moon, the shivers dance,
A snowman joins the frosty prance.
Toasty mittens and cheeks aglow,
Is it magic, or just a show?

A tumble of snowballs, a soft plop,
That snowman moves—can't make it stop!
With a scarf wrapped snug and a twinkly eye,
A chilly caper as we pass by!

Carrots giggle, as the cocoa steams,
Snowflakes gossip, or so it seems.
In winter's theater, nothing's quite clear,
Is that a waltz or the wind we hear?

A frosty chuckle fills the sky,
With every flake, the laughter flies.
In snowman tales, the tales survive,
Beneath the surface, fun is alive!

The Simmering Soul of Winter

Snowmen stand like regal kings,
Wearing hats made from old string things.
Their snowy laughter fills the air,
As they plot to give you a scare!

Round and round in little spins,
They jingle jangle like old chins.
Shivers tickle, giggles ignite,
In the pale glow of winter's light!

Soft whispers ride on icy breeze,
As snowflakes dance from chilly trees.
Did the snowman just bow to you?
In this winter world, is it true?

Hot cocoa waits, a warm delight,
While snowmen plot till morning light.
With chuckles stashed beneath their hats,
Who knew frosty fun came with such spats?

Illusions in White

In the dusk, a shimmer, a shake,
Did that snowman just take a break?
With floppy limbs in the twilight dim,
Is he dancing, or is it whim?

Frosty friends in lined-up rows,
Playing tricks, as winter knows.
A wink here, a jig there,
Snowflakes spin in the frosty air!

The whispers tickle the winter's chin,
As snowmen plot their next little grin.
In the stillness, does laughter creep?
Or is it just a snowman sleep?

As morning breaks, let’s hear the tale,
Of frosty fun that won’t grow stale.
With memories wrapped in white delight,
Who knew snowmen could be such a sight?

The Slumbering Spirit of Winter

A figure stood in frosty glee,
With carrot nose and silent plea.
Did he just blink, or was it me?
This snowman's mischief, can't you see?

A jumpy hat upon his head,
His eyes of coal, a strange thread.
With laughter ringing, just in bed,
He surely dreams of winter's spread.

His twiggy arms are all askew,
As if he wished to dance, it's true!
With every gust, he might just rue,
The frosty fun he tries to brew.

So watch him close, this winter sprite,
For in the dark, he might take flight.
And leave us all to our delight,
In giggles born of snowy night.

Shifts in the Blanket of White

In a park, the snowflakes twirl,
A snowman dances, gives a whirl.
His buttons wink, with mischief curl,
What secrets hide in winter's pearl?

He’s got some friends, a squirrel or two,
They nudge him, like pals often do.
With snowball fights, they start anew,
While all the children laugh, so true.

His snowy shoulders start to groove,
The frozen ground begins to move.
With every stomp, he starts to prove,
A sense of humor we all improve.

With giggles echoing on the breeze,
He props his bro, a fool at ease.
Together, they’re a frosty tease,
Creating fun among the trees.

Enchanted by the Winter's Breath

In the moonlight, snowflakes gleam,
A snowman stirs, or so it seems.
He whispers soft in frozen dreams,
With frosty laughter, joy redeems.

His scarf unwinds in playful cheer,
As little critters gather near.
With icy breath, he draws them near,
The winter magic, bright and clear.

Each flake that falls, he tries to catch,
With twinkling eyes, a playful match.
He’s on a mission, quite the catch,
To spread the joy, no perfect patch.

So in the night, when shadows play,
Look for the fun, don’t run away.
For he might just take you to sway,
In snowy dances, bright as day.

Shadows of the Frosted Pines

Beneath the pines, shadows sway,
A jolly figure joins the play.
With frosty antics, come what may,
He brightens up a winter's gray.

His silhouette begins to shift,
With every gust, he gives a lift.
Sudden giggles, a playful gift,
As hoots of laughter start to drift.

Snowballs fly from branch to ground,
The figure spins, with laughter found.
With friends around, they gather 'round,
As winter's magic swirls profound.

So if you see him make a move,
Don't blink or catch the snowman's groove.
With frosty cheer, he’ll make you prove,
That winter's fun is meant to soothe.

Chilling Secrets Beneath the Snow

In winter's grasp, a figure stands,
Round and jolly, made by hands.
A carrot nose, a scarf of red,
Yet whispers float from what's ahead.

The children laugh, their giggles soar,
A twinkle in the frozen core.
But what they don’t see, a twitch or two,
A frosty prankster, just for a view.

A wink of coal from beady eyes,
Crafty moves and funny lies.
With every snowball tossed and hurled,
The secrets dance in winter’s world.

Sunlight glints on snowy plains,
A mystery in jack frost’s chains.
Beneath the frost, a chuckle’s born,
As snowy pranksters greet the morn.

When Dreams Take Shape in White

A frosty dream upon the lawn,
A sculpted joy that greets the dawn.
With buttons made of stones and twine,
The laughter’s echo is divine.

Yet shadows stretch beneath the light,
Could this delight be partial fright?
Snowflakes flurry, a giggle's tease,
As chilly winds stir through the trees.

The sledders zoom, a joyful race,
While snowman grins with plump embrace.
But oh! What secret can it keep?
As children wonder, should they peek?

A bounce, a jig, a wobbly jiggle,
Warmed by fun, their spirits wiggle.
In dreams of white, they clearly see,
The snowman’s dance, wild and free.

Echoes of a Shivering Figure

Beneath the stars, a shadow creeps,
A frosty figure, laughter peeps.
With every gust, a jig it makes,
In snow drifts deep, a popcorn flakes.

With coal for eyes and hat askew,
It spins around in frosty blue.
The children squeal, in pure delight,
Is it alive? Oh, what a sight!

A dance of snowflakes in the air,
A winter wonder, unaware.
They gather close, with hearts all light,
For echoes linger through the night.

In shimmers bright, their giggles blend,
As snowmen play, and never end.
The fun unfolds with every cheer,
In frosty night, it’s plain we're near.

Frozen Laughter at Dusk

As day departs and stars ignite,
A giggling snowman greets the night.
With frosty breath, it twirls around,
In frozen glee, no frown is found.

A pipe in mouth, a cheeky grin,
As snowflakes dance on chilly skin.
The children gather, eyes aglow,
With laughter ringing through the snow.

A flick of twig, a joyful leap,
In winter's arms, the secrets keep.
With every spark that lights the sky,
The snowman winks, oh my, oh my!

In shadows deep, a funny sight,
As laughter echoes, pure delight.
In snowy dreams, their spirits roam,
For frozen laughter feels like home.

Echoes of a Snowy Mirage

In the yard stood a figure so white,
With a carrot nose and a hat so tight.
But wait! Did it twitch? Was that a wave?
Could it be a snowman, or something more brave?

Children laughed and gave a cheer,
As the snowman danced without fear.
Fluffy arms that seemed to sway,
Was this a magic snowman ballet?

With a jolly grin and a body so stout,
It rolled and tumbled, there’s no doubt.
A winter prank, oh what a sight,
Is it really alive or just frosty delight?

Sleigh bells rang in the frosty air,
As snowflakes spun with a wild flare.
The neighbors peeked and stifled their laughs,
Was it a snowman or winter gaffs?

The Wintering Enigma

In a field of glitter, bright and bold,
A figure stood, or so I'm told.
With buttons shiny, and eyes of coal,
Was it just frozen, or had it a soul?

The kids would giggle, their cheeks all aglow,
As they watched it swagger in the snow.
Puffing up proudly, it took a quick dash,
Could it be funnier than a snowball bash?

That snowman winked, or did it just blink?
Was there mischief brewing, I start to think.
A twirl, a twist, a frosty dance,
In the winter chill, oh what a chance!

So we joined in, footloose and free,
Beneath the white arch of the old maple tree.
As the snowman giggled, and we spun 'round,
The laughter echoed through the snowy ground.

Frosted Fancies

Upon the threshold of winter's charm,
A snowman stood with a frosty arm.
Did it just shiver, or maybe shake?
This icy sentinel could be a joke to make!

With candy cane stripes and a glittery hat,
It jiggled a little, how about that?
Kids gathered 'round with eyes so bright,
Could this frosted form step into the night?

In a gust of wind, it appeared to trot,
With a hodgepodge smile that couldn't be caught.
Was it alive? Did it wear a grin?
Or just a snowman with a playful spin?

As hot cocoa bubbled, and marshmallows soared,
This snowy prankster had surely adored.
And with giggles echoing all over the town,
The silly sight turned our frowns upside down.

A Glimpse of the Peculiar

Beneath the moonlight, frosty and wide,
A peculiar sight, oh, what a ride!
The snowman shuffled, not just a fake,
Could it be wise, or just a big flake?

With glow-in-the-dark buttons and a cheeky stance,
It spun and it twirled as if in a dance.
The whole village gathered, their breaths held tight,
Was this snow-kid set for a magical night?

Laughter erupted as it leapt with glee,
A snowman surprise we all had to see.
So we joined its frolic in the shimmering cold,
Winter's treasure, an enchanted unfold!

As morning broke and the sun peeked through,
The snowman was gone, oh what a view!
But memories linger of that chilly show,
Did we witness magic, or just winter's own glow?

Whispers in the Frost

A frosty figure stood so still,
With carrot nose and snowball chill.
But then a twitch caught my keen eye,
Methinks he's plotting—oh my, oh my!

The children laugh, they dart and play,
While snowflakes whisper, 'Is he okay?'
His arms are branches, his grin so wide,
But who would guess that he might hide?

Each snowy night, beneath the moon,
He sways and jiggles to a silly tune.
With every breeze, a little shake,
Is it a man or just a fake?

So gather 'round, all friends so dear,
Let's share a drink of frosty cheer!
For in this chill, one thing is clear,
The snowman dances, bringing glee near.

Shadows of the Winter Figure

In the garden, shadows play,
A snowy prankster in the fray.
With snowy cape and a cheeky grin,
What mischief could be lurking within?

Friends dare each other, 'Go say hi!'
But I just chuckle and wink my eye.
Does he just stand there, or will he bolt?
A snowman’s secret? Oh, what a jolt!

Every evening, he seems to grow,
Telling tales of winter, oh so slow.
Yet come the morning, he stands so shy,
Will he be gone by and by?

Beware the frost, my jolly mates,
For he may dance when the sun vibrates.
With every giggle the children bring,
Let’s watch the snowman do his thing!

The Frosty Illusion

A snowman prances, or so it seems,
With frosty dreams and giggly beams.
I lean in closer to catch a peek,
But he just wobbles—it's all so cheek!

His buttons glisten, eyes made of coal,
But can he scamper? Oh, that's the goal!
The world is silly in this white delight,
As whispers swirl with each frosty night.

Once in a while, he nods and grins,
As if he knows all the kid's chagrins.
With each snowflake falls a little jest,
Is he alive? Just take a guess!

So let's embrace this winter show,
With giggles, shrieks, and snowy glow.
For life with snow is pure surprise,
And in the chill, laughter will rise.

A Dance Beneath the Snowflakes

Beneath the snowflakes, what a sight,
A snowman jiggles in the moonlight bright.
With a wave of his twig, he seems to say,
'Join in the fun, let’s dance and play!'

Laughter echoes through the night,
Each snowdrift sparkling, pure delight.
His scarf unfurls like a happy tale,
Dancing wildly in the winter gale.

The kids gather round, they spin and twirl,
Caught in the magic of winter swirl.
His frosty legs kick high in the air,
Could it be true? It’s our secret affair!

So when the chill creeps in so sly,
And shadows grow as the evening goes by,
Remember the snowman, your frosty friend,
Who dances with joy, without an end.

Enchanted Chill

Amidst the flakes, a figure stands,
With a carrot nose and stick-like hands.
In the still of night, he gives a shake,
Is it my eyes, or did he awake?

A hat askew, a scarf that flaps,
He jiggles and dances, oh what a laugh!
Snowballs fly as we tease and play,
That frosty friend might steal the day.

Around him gathers a curious crowd,
Children giggle, voices loud.
Could the frost have brought him cheer?
Or is he just a prankster, here?

With every wiggle, a laugh resounds,
In this winter wonderland, joy abounds.
So here’s to the chill and all its charm,
A frosty figure with a warm heart's balm.

The Silent Sentinel of the Blizzards

Standing still, a frosty knight,
Guarding the yard through day and night.
But when I blink, he seems to sway,
Did he just move or is it play?

With twinkling eyes made of coal,
He watches over, plays his role.
But sometimes it feels like he has a plan,
To join the fun, that mischievous man.

Around him circles a snowman crew,
Each one grinning as if they knew.
Are they alive? Or just for show?
In this chilly land where wonders grow.

With every gust, they giggle and hop,
Who knew the cold could make one stop?
A sentinel of laughter under the moon,
This snowman’s charm makes winter bloom.

Dreams in White

In a world of white, where shadows bend,
Lurks a character, an unexpected friend.
With snowflakes dancing down from the sky,
I swear I saw him lift an eye!

Stitched from dreams and snowy shrouds,
He grins and twirls, among the clouds.
A wink, a nod, maybe a spin,
What a riot, let the fun begin!

The kids all gather, with sleds in tow,
Chasing snowmen, where laughter flows.
Did he just chuckle? Did I hear right?
Frosty jests in the soft starlight.

So let's embrace this gleeful quest,
With our frosty buddy, we’re truly blessed.
In the shimmer of ice, a merry sight,
Dreams unfurl in the magical night.

When the Cold Comes to Life

Once the chill dances, the magic starts,
In the hush of night, he beats the hearts.
That jolly figure, once just a mound,
Now prances 'round without a sound.

His eyes alight with snowy glee,
Wiggles and jiggles, oh my, oh me!
When winter whispers its playful tune,
The chilly rogue begins to swoon.

Around him, laughter fills the air,
Children chase him, without a care.
Is he a dancer or a snowy rogue?
With swirls and twirls, in the fog he'll stoke.

As the cold comes alive with cheer,
Who'd have thought winter could feel so dear?
In the land of frost, let's all unite,
With our groove-filled snowman, beneath the starlight.

The Winter Chronicles

In a field so white, a figure stands,
A carrot nose and stick-like hands.
He twirls and leaps, oh what a sight,
Is he dancing, or just polite?

The kids all giggle, take a look,
He strikes a pose like a storybook.
With a frosty grin and a jolly hat,
Who knew snow could be so sprat?

Then comes a gust, a thrilling breeze,
He starts to sway, oh yes, he teases.
With a cheeky wink that warms the chill,
Is that a smile or just a thrill?

As night falls down, the shadows creep,
Does he come alive while we are asleep?
With snowflakes dancing 'round his dome,
Is it crazy to think he wants to roam?

The Mystery of the Frozen Stare

In the park where the kids go play,
A frosty figure stands all day.
His glare is sharp, a frozen frown,
Is he guarding the ice or wearing a crown?

A snowball fight erupts with cheer,
But all he does is stare and leer.
With googly eyes made out of coal,
Does he have a heart or is that his role?

The laughter echoes, a jovial shout,
But the frozen guard is filled with doubt.
Does he envy the fun in the sun,
Or secretly wish he could join the run?

As shadows lengthen and laughter fades,
What secrets lie in his snowy glades?
With a wink and a nod, we bid farewell,
To the frosty figure who casts his spell.

Specters in the Snowfall

On a bright day, the snowflakes cling,
A whimsical chill, a snowman's spring.
He twirls and wobbles, oh what a sight,
Did he just prance, or was it the light?

With a scarf wrapped tight and a hat askew,
He sings a tune only snowmen know.
A tap dance here, a jiggle there,
Is he shy or just trying to share?

The children giggle, they clap their hands,
As he shimmies and shakes, oh how he stands!
With each twist and turn, they can’t help but grin,
Who knew a snowman had this much spin?

Amid the laughter and raucous play,
Did he just wink? Or was it a sway?
In the frosty air, a tale unfurls,
Of dancing snowmen in winter whirls.

What Lies Beneath the Drift

Beneath the layers, mysteries creep,
What secrets does the snowman keep?
As the children laugh and toss their balls,
The snowman's gaze seems to enthrall.

With a belly round and arms stretched wide,
Is there a mystery he can’t bide?
He jiggles and jostles, what could it be?
A snowman's wish to break free?

The wind howls softly, it’s a ghostly breeze,
Was that a move? Oh, please, oh, please!
With a chuckle hidden in snowy mounds,
Does he dream of the summer and bouncing sounds?

He stands so still, yet seems to sway,
Is he plotting mischief in his frosty way?
A wink and a nod, then back to his post,
To the hidden laughs of the icy ghost.

The Night the Snow Came Alive

In the moonlight they shook, with glee,
Dancing snowmen, oh so free!
Button eyes twinkled with delight,
Waving to us in the cold, clear night.

A carrot nose gave a charming grin,
As they spun around, let the fun begin!
Top hats tipped in a playful way,
Who knew snow could dance and sway?

The kids all stared, mouths agape,
Had winter turned into a playful cape?
With laughter ringing in the air,
They frolicked around without a care.

But as dawn broke, they froze in place,
No more movement, just a snowy face.
We laughed, wondering, did we dream?
Or was it real, that snowy team?

Enigmatic Forms in a White Wonderland

Shapes in the drifts began to sway,
Were they friends or just a play?
A snowman waved, or was it a trick?
My eyes went wide, my heart went quick.

A top hat tilted, a scarf flew by,
Were they planning an escapade, oh my!
With snowflakes giggling as they spun,
Who knew winter could be so fun?

The icy ground became their stage,
Each frosty figure engaged in the page.
With arms outstretched and grins so bright,
They put on a show, a frosty delight!

But when the sun began to rise,
They froze like statues before our eyes.
Was it magic or just a game?
In this wonderland, nothing’s the same!

Secrets Beneath the Ice

Underneath layers of frosty white,
Whispers of laughter danced in the night.
Secrets hidden in winter's embrace,
Peeking out with each chilly trace.

A snowman giggled, a snowball flew,
As winter's frost began to renew.
In frozen corners, a prankster's grin,
What secrets lurked where the cold begins?

With each puffy puff, they plotted and schemed,
While kids sat back, bewildered and dreamed.
Who knew ice could have a playful spark,
As night crept in, bright and dark?

The sun arose; they froze once more,
Yet their laughter echoing through the door.
Mysteries wrapped in snowy fluff,
Winter, you sly one, aren't you tough!

The Silent Vigil of Winter

In the stillness of a glimmering night,
Snowmen stood tall, a curious sight.
With silent poses, they took their stand,
Guarding secrets across the land.

Under a blanket, quiet and bright,
They seemed to whisper, “What a delight!”
With eyes of coal and smiles so wide,
Winter’s magic could no longer hide.

But oh, how one took a little leap,
Caught off guard while the others sleep.
A twirl and a spin, a giggle so bold,
Snowmen come alive, if only told!

Yet as dawn broke, they stood so still,
Quietly holding the night's sweet thrill.
With a chuckle, we ponder their mirth,
Do they sleep or just watch the earth?

Secrets Beneath the Snow

White blankets hide what’s underneath,
A giant’s laugh, a sneaky wreath.
Footprints lead to where they've been,
Did that carrot just grin?

The snowman jiggles, oh what a sight,
Dancing with glee in the pale moonlight.
His stick arms wave as if to say,
Let’s frolic through this winter's play.

Underneath, secrets whisper low,
Did you see that, a dance in the snow?
Laughter echoes, a chill in the air,
What’s real and what’s just a frosty scare?

So many tales the snow can weave,
Magic unfolds on this winter eve.
Mysteries chuckle, as shadows prance,
Join in the fun, give snowfall a chance.

The Eerie Stillness of December

In the hush of a winter's dream,
Snowflakes twirl, a gentle gleam.
A figure stands, but is it true?
That snowman seems to have a view.

His coal eyes sparkle with mischief bright,
Could he be plotting a snowy fright?
A sudden shiver, a breathless whoosh,
Did he just move, or was it a swoosh?

Laughter serves as a chilly song,
As we watch him bounce along.
Frosty antics, oh what a show,
With every twirl, the jests just grow.

Eerie stillness, yet giggles abound,
As frosty friends dance all around.
Who knew the snow held such great glee?
A winter's tale, come laugh with me!

Frost's Fantasia

In the twilight, a silhouette springs,
This cheerful figure almost sings.
With a wink and a laugh, did he just sway?
A frosty jig in the moon's soft ray.

The hat teeters, the nose is bold,
What other secrets has he sold?
A frosty fiesta, oh what a fate,
A snowman party we can’t replicate.

Twisting and tumbling, he shuffles around,
With every step, a giggling sound.
Could he be plotting a snowy delight?
Let’s dance with him under the starlit night.

Frosty friends, come gather near,
For in the chill, there’s laughter here.
Winter’s magic is not so grim,
With whispered jokes, let the fun begin.

Shadows that Wander

Out in the field, where shadows play,
A figure shifts in a mischievous way.
Is that a giggle or just the wind?
This snowy sentinel has a whim.

Stick arms waving, a frosty cheer,
What hidden jests are lurking here?
A hearty laugh, or was that a snort?
This playful creature seems out of sort.

With each blink, it seems to sway,
In the frosty air, they dance and play.
What a curious, amusing game,
Whispers of fun, they'll stake their claim.

Shadows wander, as the night draws near,
With each movement, comes winter cheer.
Together let’s laugh in this snowy delight,
For memories made on this chilly night.

Reflections in a Snow-Pristine World

In a blanket of white, so soft and bright,
A figure stood still, what a curious sight!
With a carrot for a nose and coal for eyes,
Did it just wiggle? Oh, what a surprise!

Children laughed loudly, their breath like steam,
Was it magic, or just a child's dream?
They dared to approach, excitement aglow,
But the snowman just chuckled, 'It's all for show!'

Snowflakes danced down like confetti so fine,
While mittens were tossed in a playful line.
With a hop and a shuffle, he joined in their game,
And the world erupted in laughter and fame!

So remember this tale of our frosty friend,
Who brought joy to the cold until winter's end.
In a world wrapped in white, where wonders convene,
Even snowmen can frolic, so funny and keen!

The Enchantment of Frigid Nights

Under the moonlight, the landscape aglow,
A snowman stood guard, but could he really know?
With buttons for a smile and a scarf wrapped tight,
Was he stretching his arms, in the chill of the night?

The children giggled, 'Look! He's up to a dance!'
As they twirled around, caught up in the prance.
With a wobble and a shimmy, he began to sway,
Their laughter echoed, 'This is quite a display!'

As snowflakes twirled in the cool evening air,
They cheered for their friend, what a whimsical fair!
For each step he took, though it felt so surreal,
Brought a joy that was vivid, a magical thrill.

So as the stars twinkled, bright in the night,
A snowman decided to join in their flight.
In a world filled with wonder, so frosty and bright,
The laughter continues, pure fun in the night!

Fables Beneath the Falling Snow

In the heart of winter, on a plain so wide,
A snowman emerged, with a laugh that he tried.
With a shimmy and shake, he began to glide,
Was he teasing the children, oh what a ride!

The frosty air sparkled, a magical tune,
As he danced with the breeze beneath the pale moon.
His top hat was tipped, a sly little bow,
The giggles erupted from every child's row!

Around him they gathered, eyes wide in delight,
While he pulled off some stunts that were truly out of sight.
With a jump and a flail, he slipped on a shoe,
Fell with a thump and the laughter just grew.

So next time you wander through a snowy expanse,
Look closely and see if you catch him in a dance.
For beneath the white cover, where whimsy does flow,
You might find a tale or two 'neath the snow!

Whims of a Winter Spirit

In a world made of flakes, where the air bites cold,
Stood a jolly snowman, if stories are told.
With a fluffy top hat and a grin on his face,
Did he just wiggle? Or was it a race?

The chill made him shiver, what a sight to behold,
With his arms all a-flap in the bright winter gold.
As snowballs flew past him, he'd tumble and roll,
Creating a scene of chaotic control!

Children erupted in fits of pure glee,
As he danced with a flair, oh what kind of spree!
With a puff and a whoosh, he opened his coat,
To reveal a surprise — it was snowflakes that float!

So gather your pals for this frosty affair,
Watch the snowman delight without any care.
For in the snowfall's embrace, where magic does start,
Lies a tale of pure joy and a warming heart!

The Winter Guardian's Dance

In the moonlight, shadows prance,
A cap on head, it starts to dance.
With a cheeky grin, it waves at me,
Oh, what a sight, so wild and free!

Snowflakes twirl in the chilly air,
As frosty feet find rhythm rare.
Twisting, turning, oh what a show,
Who knew snow could put on a glow?

Laughter echoes, the night is bright,
A jolly figure in the starlight.
With every step, the laughter grows,
Could this be where winter fun flows?

So if you hear the softest giggle,
Follow the sound and give a wiggle.
Join the dance, don’t be late,
For a winter party, oh, so great!

Frost-Kissed Mysteries Unraveled

Beneath the stars, a figure stands,
With carrot nose and stick-like hands.
A gentle sway, it nods hello,
Challenging me to join the show!

Is it a prank or magic true?
Can frost have fun? Just look at you!
With a chuckle and a frosty grin,
This winter mystery pulls me in.

Snowflakes giggle as they fall,
Whispers of mischief, winter’s call.
A playful flick, a snowball flies,
Oh, the laughter echoes, what a surprise!

Chasing dreams in the snowy night,
Each frosty breath brings sheer delight.
As the scene unfurls, my heart takes flight,
In this chilly world, everything feels right!

Glimpses of Magic in the Chill

Frosty air begins to gleam,
A figure dances, it seems to beam.
With twinkling eyes and a snow-white coat,
Spinning ‘round, it makes me float.

Through the drifts, it leaps and bounds,
Every step, a joyful sound.
Waving arms and a merry jig,
Sprinkling magic, oh so big!

Could it be mischief in the freeze?
Giggles float upon the breeze.
A snowball flies, the laughter rings,
In this frosty realm, joy springs!

So let us chase the sparkling light,
Join the fun this winter night.
For every flake is a tale to tell,
In the chill, we merrily dwell!

A Figure in the Flurries

Amidst the flurries, something spins,
A snowy grin, where fun begins.
With floppy hat and buttons bright,
It crafts a tale in the soft moonlight.

Step by step, away it sways,
Leading me through the winter maze.
A tap-dance here, a shimmy there,
With frosty joy, we romp and share.

Sprightly hops over glittering drifts,
A bundle of joy, it surely gifts.
With a twirl and skip, it beckons me,
In this winter wonder, wild and free!

Don't you blink, or you might miss,
The laughter caught in winter's kiss.
As snowflakes gather, and spirits rise,
A snowy secret beneath the skies!

Quiet Movements in the Snowfall

In the hush of night, a figure shakes,
With a carrot nose, oh, what mistakes!
Snowflakes tumble, laughter in the air,
Is it just me, or is he dancing in there?

A bobble hat, atop his head,
Seems he’s wiggling, never misled.
His coal eyes glimmer, a mischievous glance,
In this frosted world, nothing's by chance.

Could it be magic, or just my sight?
That frosty gentleman, what a delight!
With a pirouette, he spins around,
In the blanket of snow, he's homeward bound.

Laughter erupts, as we gaze in awe,
Who knew frosty friends could break the law?
In each snowy step, a playful tease,
In a winter wonderland, we can all freeze!

The Glimmer of a Wandering Heart

On a snowy eve, with stars so bright,
A figure sways under moon’s soft light.
With arms stretched wide, as if to fly,
Is it a snowman, or just a sly guy?

His scarf flutters, like whispers in dreams,
Caught in the sparkle, so funny it seems.
Dancing round, with a wink and a wave,
What secrets he holds, the frosty knave!

With a jolly jig, he moves with a flair,
Making snow angels, without a care.
In every turn, there's a giggle, a cheer,
This snowy heart brings joy everywhere!

So we join in, with laughter and glee,
Who knew a snowman could set us free?
In the winter's hush, we dance side by side,
Embracing the whimsy, on this frosty ride.

Dreams in a Snow-Spun Veil

In a blanket of white, a shadow appears,
Twirling about, fueled by snowy cheers.
With twiggy arms and a toothy grin,
He's got us all laughing, where do I begin?

Muffled giggles echo, as he takes a stance,
Wobbling and bobbing, inviting us to dance.
His round little belly shakes like a bowl,
Could this be a snowman with a lively soul?

Across the field, he rolls and he drops,
With every tumble, our laughter just hops.
In a flurry of snow, he can’t hold his ground,
What a funny sight, to see him fall down!

With each new twist, he changes his pose,
Could he be showing off? Who really knows?
But in this ballet of whims and delight,
Frosty mischief dances through the night.

A Silhouette Against a Winter's Sky

Beneath the stars, something catches the eye,
A frosty figure, under the sky.
With a floppy hat, he shuffles and plays,
Giving us giggles that last for days.

In the crisp air, a jolly jig,
Round and round, he does a big wig.
Is he alive, or just the snow’s prank?
In the moonlight, he makes quite a rank.

A tip of his hat with a cheeky smile,
He beckons us closer, it’s all worth the while.
A snowy ballet that has us all grinning,
Who knew frozen folks could be so winning?

Through the laughter, we chase through the night,
In this wintry world, everything feels bright.
So here’s to the merriment he brings with glee,
In a frozen tableau, come dance with me!

Echoes of Frosty Footsteps

In the stillness of the night,
A shadow dances, oh what a sight!
With a carrot nose and a cheeky grin,
He winks at the moon, let the mischief begin.

Laughter echoes through the chilly air,
As he hops and twirls without a care.
Snowflakes giggle as they swirl around,
With every step, a jolly sound.

The children peek from their snug beds,
Imagining dreams where the snowman treads.
Did he just jiggle? Was that a shake?
Maybe it’s just the ground that quakes!

Frosty frolics with a crazy flair,
Twisting and turning without a scare.
Come morning light, will all be still?
Or will he dance on, against his will?

Secrets Carved in Snowflakes

Whispers float on icy whirls,
As snowflakes fall and gently twirl.
They giggle softly in the night,
Sharing secrets in pure delight.

A frosty friend with a cheeky bow,
Dances beneath the moonlight's glow.
Did he just hiccup? What was that noise?
Mysteries abound, oh what a ploy!

Carrots for eyes, and a hat so fine,
He shuffles about like he’s sipping wine.
Snowflakes drop with joyous cheer,
Tickling each thought, whispering near.

As morning breaks, he freezes in place,
A playful grin on his snowy face.
Yet the footprints vanish, no sign remains,
Just a laugh carried through winter's lanes.

Murmurs in the Frigid Air

With frosty breath, the air feels alive,
Little whispers of a playful vibe.
A snowman nods, entranced by the glow,
Is that really him, or just the snow?

Under the stars, he prances and sways,
Unruly snowflakes join in the craze.
With every jig, he seems to gloat,
Wearing a scarf like a colorful coat.

The chill of night brings giggles and glee,
As he spins wildly, oh can it be?
Could he be alive, with a soul and heart?
Or just the magic of winter's art?

So we toss our hats and revel in cheer,
As the whispers of snowmen draw ever near.
Tomorrow may dawn with silence so grand,
But tonight he dances across the snow land.

Unveiling the Frozen Enigma

In the frosty depths where laughter is spun,
A snowman chuckles, oh what fun!
He rolls in the drifts, then stands up tall,
A master of tricks, he's got it all.

Hats askew and buttons misplaced,
He prances around like he's out for a chase.
Snowflakes flutter, caught off guard,
As he steals the night, it's not that hard!

Children peek out with eyes so wide,
Could he really move, with such pride?
Mystery hangs in the winter air,
As giggles escape without a care.

A laugh appears where silence reigned,
In the heart of winter, joy is maintained.
With each snow-laden step that he takes,
We unwrap the mystery, as laughter wakes.

Secrets Tucked in Frozen Corners

In the yard where the chill winds blow,
A frosty figure puts on a show.
With a carrot nose, he struts with glee,
Is that a wink, or just me?

With a floppy hat and a shiny grin,
He dances about, oh what a sin!
Snowflakes giggle as they drift and sway,
Is he plotting mischief today?

Behind the bushes, giggles abound,
As he tiptoes softly 'round and 'round.
Whispers of snowmen whisper so clear,
“Catch me if you can, when no one's near!”

Underneath the stars that glimmer bright,
Who knew a snowman could cause such fright?
With secrets tucked in frozen corners,
He’s the king of winter’s frosty mourners!

The Echo of a Whimsical Frost

Out in the yard where the frosties play,
A jolly snowman has come out to stay.
With arms of twigs and a crooked smile,
He's been a bit cheeky for quite a while!

He's stomping and hopping, in circles round,
What's that? A giggle? Oh, what a sound!
Frozen laughter fills the air,
The neighbors peek through curtains, beware!

What if he breaks into a jig?
Wouldn't that be quite the gig?
With a wiggle and a hop, he vanishes fast,
Yet tales of his antics are sure to last!

As night drapes down in shimmering glow,
Whispers of frosty tales start to flow.
A snowman's frolics, daring and bold,
Leave echoes of laughter in winter's hold.

Fragments of a Winter's Dream

In the twilight, shadows mix and dance,
A snowman sways, caught in his trance.
With buttons gleaming, he bows with flair,
Is there life in that cool frosty air?

Snowflakes tumble; they gather 'round,
As he jigs, his giggles resound.
In a swirl of white, he takes a twirl,
Who knew he could give winter a whirl?

What's this rumor, is it truly him?
Whispered stories seem so grim.
Chasing snowmen in the dark of night,
Could he really be taking flight?

With fragments of laughter glistening bright,
The snowman chuckles at the moonlight.
As dreams meld into frosty seams,
Winter whispers of magical themes.

Shadows Stretched by the Moon

Beneath the light of the silvery glow,
A sneaky snowman creeps to and fro.
With shadows long, he plots and schemes,
Is this a prank or just a dream?

Giggling softly, he snags a hat,
A fluffy scarf wrapped all around that!
Around and around, he starts to glide,
Shattering silence with laughter wide!

His frosty nose twitches with delight,
As he stirs up frosty bits of night.
Jumping over piles of gleaming white,
Daring the moon to join in the flight!

With sunlight’s return, he freezes in place,
But at night he can’t resist the chase.
In shadows stretched by the moon so bright,
A snowman’s laugh glows with pure delight.

Chilling Whimsy

In the yard where snowflakes twirl,
A frosty figure starts to curl.
With a sly grin and a wobble,
He leaps and dances on the puddle.

A carrot nose begins to twitch,
He juggles snowballs like a witch.
Round and round, he spins so fast,
Is that a snowman? Or a blast?

A scarf around his neck so bold,
Tickles the winds, or so I'm told.
With each giggle, he gives a cheer,
That frosty buddy loves to appear!

So when winter whispers soft and near,
Look close to see if he’ll appear.
You might just catch a frosty slide,
In this silly winter tide!

The Great Frosted Mirage

Amidst the flakes, a sight so rare,
A snowman’s dance in mid-air.
With twinkling eyes, he gives a wink,
And tumbles softly as we blink.

He pitches snow in quick ballet,
With leaps that make the children sway.
A frosty jig, so wild and grand,
Making snow angels on the land.

With arms outstretched, he starts to spin,
As laughter bubbles from within.
The chill in air can't hide the fun,
At sunset, he’s on the run!

Under stars, he hops and glows,
Whirling through the drifts he throws.
When morning comes, will he be there?
Or just a memory in the air?

Whispers in the Frost

In the quiet of the snowy night,
I swear I saw a frosty sight.
A snowman grinning, quite awake,
Dancing merry for winter's sake.

With twirling arms, and such a flair,
He glides and laughs without a care.
Mittens off, he jumps around,
No frozen fate will hold him down!

'Catch me if you can!' he shouts,
While spinning flakes like swirling sprout.
A playful ghost of winter's womb,
Sharing giggles in the gloom.

So if you hear the crunch of snow,
And giggles that begin to grow,
Peek outside to see him there,
Playing peek-a-boo in the cold air!

Shadows of Winter's Play

Beneath the moon's soft silvery glow,
A snowman prances on the snow.
With shadowy limbs that leap and sway,
He plays hide and seek till break of day.

His hat sits crooked, in a flurry,
He slips and slides without a worry.
From drifts to flurried jumps he bounds,
Creating laughter all around.

As footprints fade in morning light,
Who's there to say he's out of sight?
A ghost of frosty whimsy's song,
In winter's heart where he belongs.

So when the cold begins to tease,
And playful snow fills up the trees,
Join the frosty brigade with glee,
For winter's whimsy calls to thee!

The Last Breath of Winter Wonderland

In the white expanse, a figure takes a stand,
With a carrot nose, it looks quite grand.
But wait, a twitch, could it be alive?
A frosty friend that's trying to thrive?

The kids all giggle, hiding behind trees,
As the snowman wiggles, and flops with ease.
His hat keeps tipping, his scarf in a whirl,
A winter dance, oh how they twirl!

The sun brings warmth, a melting affair,
Is he just dreaming? Oh, do we dare?
With a playful grin, he takes a hop,
Too silly to think he might ever stop!

As winter whispers a final goodbye,
Our frosty friend twirls, under the sky.
With a belly laugh made of snow and ice,
He giggles away, isn’t life nice?

Dancing Between the Snowflakes

Snowflakes fall as music plays,
A snowman grins, in frosty arrays.
He jiggles and bounces, quite out of place,
In his world of white, he's found his grace.

With twirls and spins, he slides down hills,
Making the most of winter's thrills.
The wind whispers secrets, with magical charms,
While he waves to the trees with his snowy arms.

Kids gather 'round with shouts of delight,
As he breaks into dance, what a comical sight!
He tiptoes and shuffles, oh what a show,
A snowy ballet, stealing the glow.

But as the sun peeks, the groove starts to fade,
The snowman chuckles, "What a grand parade!"
With a wink and a nod, he takes a bow,
"Catch me next winter, I'll show you how!"

Shimmering Legends of the Cold

In the hush of the night, a glow starts to sway,
A snowman smiles, ready to play.
With icicle arms and a giggle so bright,
He's the king of the frosty, a whimsical sight.

Legends are told of his magical grace,
Rumor has it he can dance all over the place.
He hops and he bounces on powdery ground,
Creating a symphony of laughter around.

As shadows lengthen, and the moon beams high,
He twirls in the stillness 'neath starry sky.
With a wiggle and jiggle, he starts to groove,
A frosty old legend determined to move!

But with dawn's first light, he waves his goodbye,
And slips in the mist, like a whispering sigh.
"Just a tale for the ages, till winter returns,
When the snowman dances, and the whole world churns!"

Enigmas in the Winter's Glow

In the meadow of snow, a riddle unfolds,
A snowman with antics, quite daring and bold.
Wobbling and jiggling, what's going on?
Is it magic or mischief, from dusk until dawn?

His buttons a-twinkle, a mischievous gleam,
He tumbles and tumbles, like a snowball dream.
With a flurry of laughter, he plays hide and seek,
Among frosted branches, cheeky and sleek.

The whispers of winter carry his jest,
As children peer closely, enthralled by the quest.
He nods and he winks, then strikes a pose,
“Catch me if you can!”, only winter knows.

So gather ‘round closely, in the chilly embrace,
For enigmas bring joy in this wintry space.
With a clap and a swirl, the frosty tale grows,
As the joyous snowman, forever bestows!

Flickers of Life in the Snow

In a field of white, strange sights arise,
A carrot nose twitches, much to my surprise.
Snowballs grow legs, and they scamper about,
Chasing after snowflakes, giggling with shout.

A scarf wrapped tightly, it starts to sway,
Was that a wink? Oh, what a funny display!
Snowmen in motion, quite the comical scene,
Who knew frosty figures could be so keen?

Just when I thought they were stiff as a board,
They break into dance, my laughter, they hoard.
With a hop and a skip, and a frosty pirouette,
These chilly characters, I'll never forget.

So when winter arrives with its icy embrace,
Watch out for the snowmen, with smiles on their face.
For hidden beneath, in the chills and the fog,
Mischievous snowfolk may spring from the bog!

The Playful Specter of Frost

On a sunlit morning, all is sublime,
But hold on a minute, all's not as prime!
There's a snowman grinning, it's moving, no doubt,
Riding on ice skates, with a playful sprout.

With arms made of branches, they wave and they cheer,
Shouting for joy as they glide without fear.
Each swirl of their figure, so goofy and bright,
Makes me wonder if they're real, oh, what a sight!

A top hat that tumbles, a broom that can dance,
I start to giggle, could this be my chance?
To join in their frolic, to twirl in the snow,
Who knew winter brought such delight in tow?

As laughter erupts and the snowflakes conspire,
These frosty companions, they lift my heart higher.
With each silly move, they bring warmth to the cold,
These playful specters of frost, such stories unfold!

White Whispers of the Unknown

Amidst the white powder, strange things seem to stir,
A foot here, a hand there, oh, what could occur?
Whispers of frosty figures begin to swirl,
With marshmallow laughter, as snowflakes twirl.

Eyes made of coal are glimmering bright,
Are they watching closely, in the tranquil night?
I hear a strange chuckle on the wind's chilly breath,
Could it be the snowfolk, playing tricks with death?

Wobbling and bobbling, they craft quite the plight,
Each flurry a giggle, each snowdrift a fright.
With leaps and with bounds, they play peek-a-boo,
Bringing me laughter, while hiding from view.

In silence they move, with whimsical grace,
I cheer on their antics, this merry snow race.
For winter holds secrets, in each snowy flake,
And snowmen in motion, oh, what fun they make!

The Chilling Dance of the Unknown

When night blankets all, and the moon starts to rise,
Something stirs in the snow, to my wide-open eyes.
There's a jiggle and wiggle, a laugh oh so sweet,
A snowman in moonlight, doing the elite.

With twirls on the ice, they glide to and fro,
While other snowballs join in on the show.
I lose track of time, caught up in their spree,
As they whirl and they twirl, just wild as can be.

Their arms made of branches, resembling a band,
Creating a ruckus, all unplanned and unplanned.
With snow flying high, oh what a delight,
These frosty fans of fun dance deep in the night.

As laughter echoes sharp in the crisp, wintry air,
I join in their revels, without any care.
For the chilling dance of those strangers unknown,
Fills my heart with cheer, as we share this cold throne!